THE
EMPLOYMENT LAW
POCKETBOOK WITHDRAWN

By Malcolm Martin and Tricia Jackson

Drawings by Phil Hailstone

"All managers have to work within the restrictions of employment law. This book outlines the law and offers some practical solutions. Essential reading for all managers. HR staff will find this book an extremely useful checklist of key employment law requirements and a source of practical advice in how to meet them."
Olga Aikin, Senior Partner, Aikin Driver Partnership

"A well written, concrete and practical guide through the minefield of HR legislation. This invaluable tool provides guidance and reassurance for all managers."
Sue Murray, Director, Mango Marketing

Published by:
Management Pocketbooks Ltd
Laurel House, Station Approach,
Alresford, Hants SO24 9JH, U.K.
Tel: +44 (0)1962 735573
Fax: +44 (0)1962 733637
E-mail: sales@pocketbook.co.uk
Website: www.pocketbook.co.uk

First published 2004.
This edition published 2006.

© Malcolm Martin and Tricia Jackson 2004.

British Library Cataloguing-in-Publication
Data – A catalogue record for this book is
available from the British Library.

ISBN - 13   978 1 903776 44 5
ISBN - 10   1 903776 44 9

Design, typesetting and
graphics by **efex ltd**.   Printed in U.K.

CONTENTS

CONTENTS

INTRODUCTION

The idea for this book arose because a Personnel Manager asked us to recommend a book that would give a brief summary of employment law for her supervisors and managers.

So we hope that this book will prove invaluable as an initial guide for all frontline managers, whether you are an owner-manager of a small business or a supervisor in a large plc. We hope that the general guidance here will alert you to what you need to know and set you off on the right path. Please keep in mind that, in many cases, you will need to know a lot more than this book can tell you and it is very important that you check for changes and special circumstances.

Some tips on finding further advice are provided in the first section and there is a list of further reading at the end of the book.

We applaud all those who take on the responsibility of managing others. We wish you sound relationships and just rewards.

Acknowledgements

We would like to acknowledge the contribution of all those with whom we have worked: clients, delegates on workshops and associates; they have contributed to our knowledge.

Carole Moseley gave us the idea of this book and deserves particular thanks.

Although all errors are our responsibility, we wish to thank Les Frankish for his specific help with the section on Health and Safety. Last, but not least, thanks to our respective partners, Christina and David for being supportive as ever.

CONTRACTS OF
EMPLOYMENT

CONTRACTS OF EMPLOYMENT

WHERE TO GET ADVICE

A good knowledge of relevant law will make life much easier for anyone who manages people. Let this book be your guide. Then remember that the best advice you might ever receive is to listen to advice! We advocate that you supplement the guidance here with good advice and always do so when in any doubt.

- Human resources, legal or personnel departments should be the first port of call
- ACAS run free helplines for employers and employees – see the phonebook
- Some professional bodies and employer organisations run helplines
- Local law firms may run helplines – check terms and be sure they have an employment specialist first
- Continually updated reference books, employers' briefings and law-lines are widely available from Croners, Jordans, CIPD and others – search the web

Law is primarily made up of Acts, Regulations, Codes of Practice, and past cases. The latter also help to define good practices that courts use to determine reasonableness. Law changes continually and this pocketbook is only a broad guide for managers, based on UK legislation. Please bear in mind that the law described in this book is simplified, and will not cover everything. Be wary!

CONTRACTS OF EMPLOYMENT

CIVIL LAW

Civil law is used when one person '**wrongs**' another. Scott services Emma's car. Emma drives it out of the garage and the wheel falls off. Emma expects Scott to pay for the damage; if he refuses she can sue him in a civil court, such as the County Court.

Similar applies in **employment**. Careless Ltd hires Jack who has an accident at work. Jack can sue Careless Ltd for personal injuries.

Civil law works around **contracts** between people or organisations.

As soon as Careless Ltd gets the claim it fires Jack, on the spot. This is **wrongful** dismissal. Jack can claim damages because Careless Ltd has broken the contract. At the least, Jack is entitled to notice pay.

There are three categories of employment contract: employees, workers and self-employed. **Employees** get special protection rights and some of these special rights also apply to **workers**. Some people may have **self-employed** contracts but they have to be in business on their own account to qualify. These are often referred to as 'genuinely' self-employed, to distinguish them from workers.

CONTRACTS OF EMPLOYMENT

EMPLOYEE, WORKER OR GENUINELY SELF-EMPLOYED?

It is important to decide into which category a person falls. It is not easy because people often span factors across categories. The ideas below help you to decide, although they do not define every case. If a person does not clearly fall into one category, seek advice.

Employee	Worker	Genuinely self-employed
Contract of service (ie to serve)	S/he does the work personally	Contracts for services - you are their customer
You pay by PAYE	You pay on invoice	You pay on invoice
S/he is not VAT registered	S/he may be VAT registered	Prepares business accounts
You set the hours	Either may set hours of work	S/he sets hours
S/he can't decline work	S/he can decline work	Can assign work to others
You can expect work	You cannot expect work	No right to expect work
You provide written employment particulars	Contract may not be in writing	Contracts for each piece of work; could be written
S/he subject to discipline	Complaint or discipline	Liable to complaints
S/he uses company equipment	May use own equipment	Uses own equipment
For an indefinite time	Usually fixed time	Contract by service, not time

CONTRACTS OF EMPLOYMENT

MAKING A CONTRACT

Whatever the category, when making a contract the principles are largely the same:

Offer:	You can attach conditions to an offer, such as receiving references you find satisfactory. Put time limits on acceptance or withdraw the offer if it is not accepted. Watch for inadvertent offers such as *'Can you start on Monday?'*
Acceptance:	Offers can be accepted by actions, eg the applicant arrives for work!
Certainty:	Neither offer nor acceptance needs to be in writing, but there has to be some certainty about what has been agreed, so it avoids doubt if they are written.
Consideration:	There has to be something for both parties, typically wages in return for work. Voluntary work is not covered here; take advice.
Intention:	Employees, workers and self-employed invariably intend to make legally binding contracts, but be careful when employing family members.
Consent:	You cannot use duress to secure acceptance of your offer!
Legality:	Don't pay people from petty cash – neither you, nor they, will be protected.
Capacity:	When making an offer, make sure you have the authority to do so.

CONTRACTS OF EMPLOYMENT

WRITTEN PARTICULARS

Once employed by you for four weeks, an employee has the right to a written statement on the following (and it could cost you in a tribunal case if you don't have one). Note that certain further details are required for employees working outside the UK for over a month.

In one main document:	Possibly in separate documents:
• Names of employer and employee • Date when employment began, and when continuous employment began • Scale or rate of remuneration or method of calculation • Intervals at which remuneration is paid • Terms and conditions relating to hours of work (including normal working hours) • Holiday entitlement (including any entitlement to accrue holiday pay) • Job title or brief job description • Place of work	• Injury, sickness, and sick pay terms • Pensions and pension schemes • Period of notice each party must give, or how long temporary employment is likely to last, or the termination date for a fixed-term contract • Collective agreements which directly affect terms and conditions • Details of the statutory discipline and grievance procedures, including with whom an employee raises a grievance or appeals against a disciplinary decision

CONTRACTS OF EMPLOYMENT

TERMS AND CONDITIONS

EMPLOYEE HANDBOOKS

Most employers provide details of sick pay, discipline and grievance procedures in an employee handbook.
As a manager you need to be familiar with what this handbook contains.

Payment processes
Sickness and absence
Disciplinary procedure
Redundancy
E-mail and internet
Drugs and alcohol
Family friendliness
Restraint on work
Hours of work
Health and safety
Grievances
Company benefits

Compassionate leave
Maternity leave and pay
Intellectual property
Public duties
Holiday and leave
Data protection
Disciplinary rules
Capability/performance
Smoking
Harassment and bullying
Company cars
Trade union agreements

If you need to prepare policies or procedures, use the above as a checklist. You can get content guidance from some of the references in the Further Reading section.

CONTRACTS OF EMPLOYMENT

IMPLIED CONTRACTUAL TERMS

In addition to whatever you include in written particulars, or an employee handbook, **employees** are entitled to many statutory rights and **workers** are entitled to most of them also, aside from unfair dismissal. They are 'implied into every contract' whether or not they are written in. Here are a few, though there are others that apply in specific cases. If you even think that you *could* be infringing someone's rights, take further advice, perhaps from an HR department. You will also find further details in later sections of this book.

- Period of notice (one week for up to two years' service, then one week for every year worked to a maximum of 12 weeks)
- Working Time Regulations (hours of work, paid leave, breaks, night work)
- National minimum wage
- Redundancy pay
- Maternity pay, paternity pay and adoption pay
- Discipline and grievance procedures
- Rights under the Health and Safety at Work Act
- Rights to equal treatment with other employee groups (eg part-time compared to full-time)

CONTRACTS OF EMPLOYMENT

FURTHER IMPLIED TERMS

COMMON LAW/CUSTOM AND PRACTICE

Common law (that is, law derived from court decisions rather than Parliament) gives your employees other rights that are also implied into the contract of employment.

Trust and confidence is an important example. If you breach trust and confidence (eg by reporting an employee to the police without sound cause, or by reducing their pay) the employee might regard the contract as broken. They could sue for wrongful dismissal and, subject to service, claim unfair dismissal.

Duty of care is another example. Employees have the right to expect you to take due care of their physical and mental welfare.

In these cases it is for a court to decide if common law rights have been breached, though there is much guidance available to professional legal advisers from case law.

Employees can also acquire rights from custom and practice. For example, the tea-break that has always been taken will become a right, due to custom and practice.

CONTRACTS OF EMPLOYMENT

INDUCTION

Good induction can protect you from misunderstandings and it reinforces the relationship between you and your employee.

An employee handbook will help, but make sure that your induction includes:

- Health and safety – any particular or general hazards that apply to the job
- Disciplinary rules that could lead to warnings or dismissal
- General policies and procedures on issues like smoking or taking leave
- Policies that might have specific application in the context of the job such as data protection or internet access
- Explanations of procedures where non-compliance may be a disciplinary matter, eg sickness reporting
- Guidance as to where to find further information relating to the employment

Check understanding as you go through the process. Make a record of what you have covered. Signatures can be helpful, but *understanding* matters more.

Avoiding discrimination

AVOIDING DISCRIMINATION

INTRODUCTION

UK employment law provides protection from discrimination in the workplace on a number of grounds. As a result of European Union initiatives, these are being added to all the time. The majority of these grounds are covered below.
Protection from discrimination covers:

- Pre-employment
- During employment
- The termination of employment
- Post-employment

Unlike unfair dismissal, there is no service requirement for a discrimination claim. Also, there are no limits to the amount of compensation that an employment tribunal can award an employee making a successful claim of discrimination against you.

PEOPLE MANAGEMENT PRACTICES

You will need to ensure that you do not discriminate against protected groups in the following areas:

Pre-employment
- at the job analysis and advertising stages
- in your recruitment and selection practices
- in establishing the terms of the employment contract, such as the hours of work and annual salary
- in the induction of new employees

During employment
- in the contents and intent of your company policies and procedures
- in offering access to/provision of training and development opportunities
- in promotion decisions, in managing performance issues and in handling grievances
- in making changes to terms and conditions of employment and in the allocation of rewards

The termination of employment
- in dismissal decisions including selecting staff for redundancy
- in the payment of final monies and the provision of employment references

Post-employment
- eg failing to provide a reference for an ex-employee who has made a complaint about discrimination

(17)

AVOIDING DISCRIMINATION

THE LEGISLATION

The main pieces of legislation (as amended by later statutes/regulations) are the:

Sex Discrimination Act (SDA) 1975

Race Relations Act (RRA) 1976

Disability Discrimination Act (DDA) 1995

Part-time Workers (Prevention of Less Favourable Treatment) Regulations 2000

Equal Pay Act (EPA) 1970

In the following section we will be covering statute law, case law and good practices.

THE LEGISLATION IN SUMMARY

In simple terms:

- It is unlawful for managers to take into account a person's gender, marriage, colour, race, nationality, ethnic or national origin, disability or hours of work in employment decisions (see the rest of this section for details of other protected groups)

- Workers must be protected from victimisation, harassment and bullying in the workplace

- Women and men are entitled to equal pay for equal work, regardless of the number of hours worked

- There is protection from discrimination on the grounds of pregnancy or maternity

- Equal pay claims, and those of discrimination and unfair dismissal are made to employment tribunals

DIRECT DISCRIMINATION

Direct discrimination concerns treating a person on one of the prohibited grounds less favourably than others would be treated in similar circumstances.

For example:

- Conduct that demeans others, especially by reason of sex, race or disability
- Historic divisions into 'men's jobs' and 'women's jobs'
- Excuses for non-selection (eg claiming that there are no facilities for women)

20

AVOIDING DISCRIMINATION

INDIRECT DISCRIMINATION

Indirect discrimination occurs when a provision, criterion or practice is applied to everyone but which, whether intentionally or not, adversely affects people of a particular group, eg racial group.

An example of **indirect race discrimination** would be a job advertisement which states that GCSE English is an essential job requirement, as this would adversely affect applicants who were educated overseas.

An example of **indirect sex discrimination** would be imposing a minimum height requirement for a job vacancy, as this would have an adverse impact on female applicants.

VICTIMISATION, HARASSMENT AND BULLYING

Workers are protected from unlawful discrimination, namely victimisation, harassment and bullying.

Victimisation occurs when you subject an employee to detrimental treatment on the grounds that he or she has raised an internal grievance or made an employment tribunal claim about denial of a statutory right, or assisted another employee in so doing. An example would be a refusal to promote that employee.

Harassment occurs where, on one of the prohibited grounds, someone engages in unwanted conduct which has the purpose of violating the other person's dignity or creating an intimidating, hostile, degrading, humiliating or offensive environment. Examples range from physical assault to exclusion from normal workplace conversations.

Bullying is less precisely defined and may not always be related to one of the prohibited grounds. It can take many forms but usually involves the intentional intimidation or belittling of an individual. It may arise from the misuse of managerial power or authority. Not only may employees pursue employment tribunal claims in such instances but they may have grounds for personal injury claims where stress has resulted from the bullying.

DISABILITY DISCRIMINATION

There are two main types:

- Direct disability discrimination, ie less favourable treatment because of a person's disability. An example would be where you turn down an applicant with a severe facial disfigurement for a clerical position because colleagues may feel uncomfortable in his or her presence. This can never be justified so will be unlawful

- Disability-related discrimination, ie discriminatory treatment related to a person's disability, which may be objectively justified and is not trivial or minor. In the above example, if the job in question were modelling cosmetics then this might be considered a justifiable reason for rejecting the disabled applicant

There is no concept of indirect discrimination in cases of disability but, unlike other equal opportunities areas, positive discrimination is permissible.

DISABILITY – REASONABLE ADJUSTMENTS

You are also required to make reasonable adjustments so that disabled applicants or workers are not put at any substantial disadvantage, eg:

- Changes to premises
- Changes to job duties
- Adjustments to working hours
- The provision of equipment and/or support

An example of a reasonable adjustment might be providing an adapted telephone for someone with a hearing impairment.

AVOIDING DISCRIMINATION

ATYPICAL WORKERS

Part-time workers – have the right to equal treatment with full-timers. This covers a range of pay elements such as pensions, severance pay, access to promotion and training opportunities, and sickness benefits. They also acquire unfair dismissal and redundancy pay rights after the same periods of service as full-timers.

Fixed term workers – have equality of treatment with permanent counterparts on similar terms to those stated above.

Flexible working arrangements – your employees with 26 weeks' continuous service, who are parents of children under six or of disabled children under 18, are able to apply for, say, a change to working hours, times of working and place of work. You will need to respond within defined timescales, and any decision to reject the request must be for a permitted reason, eg burden of additional costs, inability to reorganise work amongst existing staff or the need to recruit additional staff.

OTHER PROTECTED GROUPS

Statutory legislation provides protection from discrimination (including direct, indirect, victimisation and harassment) in the following **instances**:

Sexual orientation – it is unlawful for you to discriminate against workers and job applicants on the grounds of sexual orientation or perceived sexual orientation.

Civil partnerships – you must provide the same employment benefits to employees with civil partners as to employees who are married, eg pension rights, life insurance and perks.

Religion or belief – it is unlawful for you to discriminate against workers and job applicants on the grounds of religion or belief.

Age – from October 2006, it will be unlawful to discriminate against workers and job applicants on the grounds of their age or perceived age. This change will impact on a wide range of employment policies, procedures and practices, eg recruitment practices through to retirement and pensions policies.

OTHER PROTECTED GROUPS

Statutory legislation provides protection from discrimination in the following instances:

Offenders with spent convictions – a person who has become a rehabilitated person may lawfully conceal their spent conviction from you if you are an employer or prospective employer.

Trade union membership or non-membership – it is unlawful for you to refuse a person employment on grounds related to trade union membership or non-membership. Employees also have the right not to suffer detriment for trade union membership or activities. This is a complicated area but an example of unlawful discrimination would be where a trade union representative is selected for redundancy because managers view him or her as a troublemaker following recent industrial action.

Transsexualism – you would be guilty of unlawful discrimination if you treated a transsexual employee or job applicant less favourably than others.

OTHER PROTECTED GROUPS

Whistleblowers – this is the term used to describe employees who perceive a wrongdoing at work and report it to an outsider. You must not dismiss or otherwise discriminate against an employee who has made a protected disclosure. The types of disclosure covered by the Act concern criminal offences, failure to comply with legal obligations, miscarriages of justice, health and safety risks and environmental damage.

Employees who are asserting a statutory right – it is automatically unfair to dismiss (including selection for redundancy) an employee who, for example:

- Queries an unlawful deduction from his or her wages

- Wishes to exercise his or her right to be accompanied at a disciplinary hearing

- Exercises his or her right to take parental leave

AVOIDING DISCRIMINATION

GOOD PRACTICES
POLICIES AND PROCEDURES

A good starting point is for you to put into place a robust **equal opportunities policy and procedure** which is integrated with non-discriminatory policies and procedures on:

Recruitment and selection	**Flexible working arrangements**
Training and development	**'Time off' arrangements**
Discipline and capability	**Job evaluation and equal pay**
Grievances	**Performance management**
Redundancy including selection criteria	**Employee reward**

AVOIDING DISCRIMINATION

GOOD PRACTICES
MANAGEMENT ACTIONS

Written policies and procedures must be backed up with good management practices.
For instance:

- Keep accurate records of the reasons for all your employment decisions

- Make opportunities for training and development equally accessible to full-time, part-time and fixed term workers

- Time training events so that they suit workers with outside commitments

- Base your selection decisions on 'suitability for the job' only

- Ensure that the allocation of rewards such as performance-related pay relate to fair and objective criteria

- Seek employee involvement in establishing a dress code so that differing cultures and needs are taken account of

- Provide honest and justifiable references for employees and ex-employees (see section on Control and Administration for more information)

AVOIDING DISCRIMINATION

POSITIVE ACTION

You may wish to go further and take positive action to redress imbalances in the profile of job applicants or your workforce. Positive action includes:

- Monitoring applications and establishing the profile of the existing workforce to see how it compares with the local population
- Advertising job vacancies in ethnic minority publications and/or welcoming applications from under-represented groups
- Ensuring that your premises are user-friendly for a range of disabled people
- Carrying out awareness training for managers and all workers
- Being proactive in providing flexible working arrangements regarding hours and location of work and career breaks
- Providing help with childcare arrangements
- Organising special needs training such as management training for 'women only' groups or pre-employment courses for ethnic minorities

Positive action is not **positive discrimination**; discrimination is not allowed at the point where an employment decision is taken. Positive disability descrimination is the only exception.

MAKING COMPLAINTS/TACKLING OFFENDERS

In these two very important areas, you must ensure that workers are encouraged to make complaints about perceived unfair treatment via your company's **grievance procedure**. Such complaints must be treated seriously by your managers and fully investigated before decisions are reached.

You may wish to provide separate procedures for more serious complaints such as **bullying**, **harassment** and those which involve potential **whistleblowing** issues.

If the complaint appears to be justified, then your managers must follow the **disciplinary procedure** in tackling offenders.

See the section on Workplace Problems for more guidance.

CONTROL AND ADMINISTRATION

INTRODUCTION

As covered in the first chapter, you are obliged to provide employees with written particulars, which set out their main terms and conditions of employment.

Among the items that must be covered are:

- Pay
- Hours of work
- Holiday entitlement

Legislation has established statutory entitlements in these areas. The main requirements are summarised in the following pages, but the legislation is very complex so you should seek advice if you are concerned about meeting your obligations.

You must also ensure that any personal data that you hold on job applicants, workers and ex-workers is managed so as to comply with data protection legislation (see pages 43-45).

NATIONAL MINIMUM WAGE

The National Minimum Wage (NMW) Act 1998 provides a minimum wage for all workers, eg:

- Employees
- Apprentices
- Casual workers
- Employees of sub-contractors
- Agency staff
- Homeworkers

There are a number of exclusions from the Act, including:

- Those who are genuinely self-employed
- Workers under 16
- Apprentices under 26 in the first year of their apprenticeship
- Non-employed trainees on government funded training schemes
- Students on sandwich courses
- Teacher trainees placed in schools
- People who live and work as part of a family, eg au pairs

CONTROL AND ADMINISTRATION

NATIONAL MINIMUM WAGE

TYPES OF WORK

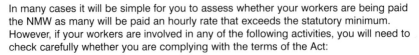

In many cases it will be simple for you to assess whether your workers are being paid the NMW as many will be paid an hourly rate that exceeds the statutory minimum. However, if your workers are involved in any of the following activities, you will need to check carefully whether you are complying with the terms of the Act:

- Piecework
- Commission work
- Night working
- Home working
- Waiting time
- Travel time
- On call

- Stand-by
- Casual work
- Unmeasured work (where there are tasks to be done but no set hours or times to do them)

The rules and calculations of pay and hours differ depending on the type of work.

NATIONAL MINIMUM WAGE
KEEPING RECORDS

Individuals have the right to apply to a court or tribunal for non-payment of the NMW.

You must keep sufficient records to show that you are paying your workers the NMW for all the activities they are engaged in on your behalf. In most cases, existing pay records will meet these requirements, but where you employ atypical workers (see page 36), you will need to be able to demonstrate that the NMW has been paid wherever it is applicable.

There are various criminal offences under the NMW Act including:

- Keeping false records
- Refusing to pay the NMW
- Obstructing an enforcement officer

Each offence is liable to a fine of up to £5,000.

CONTROL AND ADMINISTRATION

WORKING TIME REGULATIONS

The Working Time Regulations (WTR) 1998 regulate five main areas of employment:

- The length of the working week
- Night working
- Dangerous patterns of work
- Entitlement to rest periods and breaks
- Entitlement to paid annual leave

We will cover each of these requirements in brief, but you should refer to the Further Reading section at the end of the book for more help.

You will need to keep adequate records on your workers' hours of work, etc, in order to comply with the regulations.

Please note that there is additional protection for young workers.

CONTROL AND ADMINISTRATION

WORKING TIME REGULATIONS

MAXIMUM WORKING WEEK

The maximum weekly working time is stated to be '*an average of 48 hours for each 7 days*' in any applicable reference period. The reference period is normally 17 weeks but that can be increased to 26 weeks or 52 weeks, depending on the circumstances.

You must take overtime into account in such a calculation. The averaging system means that the 48 hours maximum can be exceeded in some weeks so long as there is a corresponding shortfall in others.

Currently, employees can voluntarily opt out of the 48-hour week, but this provision is being reviewed and is likely to be removed or its use restricted in the future.

CONTROL AND ADMINISTRATION

WORKING TIME REGULATIONS
NIGHT WORKING/PATTERN OF WORK

If you employ night workers, you should note that their hours of work in any applicable reference period should not exceed an average of 8 hours for each 24 consecutive hours, calculated over a reference period.

A night worker is defined as a worker who normally works *'three or more hours of his/her daily working time at night'*. Night-time will usually be the period between 11.00pm and 6.00am.

There is some flexibility in the application of this requirement but essentially there are significant implications for any of your workers who regularly work at night.

Additionally, where the work involves special hazards or heavy physical or mental strain, an absolute maximum of eight hours can become applicable. Adequate rest periods, over and above those detailed below, may also be required.

WORKING TIME REGULATIONS
REST PERIODS/BREAKS

Again, the regulations are complicated, but essentially adult workers are entitled to a:

- Daily rest period of not less than 11 consecutive hours in each 24-hour period during which they work for you
- Weekly rest period of not less than 24 hours in each 7-day period of work
- Rest break of 20 minutes where daily working time is more than 6 hours

Thus, there is protection for workers who might feel compelled to work, say:

- Back-to-back 8-hour shifts in a manufacturing establishment
- A 7-day week in a 24/7 call centre environment
- Without a break due to staff shortages in a customer service role

CONTROL AND ADMINISTRATION

WORKING TIME REGULATIONS

ANNUAL LEAVE

You may well already provide paid annual leave to your employees in excess of the statutory minimum, but the entitlement for all workers is:

- Four weeks' paid leave for each leave year
- At the rate of a week's pay in respect of each week of leave

This right cannot be excluded or modified in any way, as the aim is to encourage workers to take time off from work.

You will need to ensure that you are complying with this regulation for all workers, eg:

- Temporary
- Fixed term
- Casual workers

Also, if you employ part-time workers, you should note that their annual leave entitlement must be calculated on a pro-rata basis to the entitlement (including public holidays) of your full-time workers. This applies regardless of whether you pay at the level of, or in excess of, the statutory annual leave entitlement.

DATA PROTECTION

SOME KEY POINTS

All **personal data** must be managed in accordance with the Data Protection Act 1998.

- Data does not need to be private to be deemed **personal data**, eg a person's address may be in the telephone book, but it is still personal data

- Information that is held about a living identifiable person is personal data but it has to have them as the focus and to be biographical to a significant extent. All records, including paper, microfiche, electronic files and recorded tape, are relevant

- **Sensitive data** includes, among others, information on physical and mental health, disabilities, ethnic origin and religious belief. Storing it usually requires the employee's explicit permission

- Employees have rights to access to information held about them (including interview notes)

- Employers need to designate a person in charge of data protection and comply with certain data protection principles (see next page). Failure may lead to a criminal offence being committed

CONTROL AND ADMINISTRATION

DATA PROTECTION PRINCIPLES

There are eight data protection principles and all employers need to comply. Under the principles, personal data must be:

1. Processed fairly and lawfully
2. Processed for limited purposes and not in any manner incompatible with those purposes
3. Adequate, relevant and not excessive
4. Accurate
5. Not kept for longer than is necessary
6. Processed in line with data subjects' rights
7. Secure
8. Not transferred to countries that don't protect personal data adequately

DATA PROTECTION CODE

The principles can be complex to translate into practice. An Employment Practices Data Protection Code helps managers to comply. It has four parts:

Recruitment and selection – job applications and pre-employment vetting
Employment records – collecting, storing, disclosing and deleting records
Monitoring at work – monitoring use of eg telephone or e-mail systems and tachographs
Medical information – occupational health, medical testing, certain screening

The Code, available on the data protection website, contains detailed guidance on practices and procedures and very useful checklists. In addition employers need to provide:

- A data protection policy
- Data protection procedures
- Guidance for employees
- Training for employees
- Disciplinary rules for failure to comply with the policy

EMPLOYMENT REFERENCES

KEY POINTS AND GOOD PRACTICE

'Establish, at the time a worker's employment ends, whether or not the worker wishes references to be provided to future employers.' (Data Protection Code of Practice).

Employers are legally responsible for references given in their name so you should note that employees, or ex-employees, may be able to obtain access to their references from the organisations to which they were sent.

However, if you receive a reference, take steps to protect the identity of the author of the reference because the author is entitled to confidentiality.

'Workers should be able to challenge information that they consider to be inaccurate or misleading.' (Data Protection Code of Practice).

Openness with references is good practice. Ensure that references are only sent to reputable businesses at known addresses. References must be *'true, accurate and fair'* but need not be *'full and comprehensive'*. Adverse references must quote only established facts and never be negligent.

HEALTH AND SAFETY

HEALTH AND SAFETY

INTRODUCTION

According to the Health and Safety Executive (HSE), each year in Britain 200-300 people lose their lives at work and over 150,000 non-fatal accidents are reported. A further 2 million people are suffering from ill-health caused or made worse by their current or past work.

Health and safety legislation in the UK has grown in volume and become more detailed and prescriptive over the last 40 years. This is mainly as a result of membership of the European Union.

In this book we cannot hope to cover all the legislative requirements that will apply to your workplace, but the main provisions are summarised. See also the Further Reading section at the back of the book.

HEALTH AND SAFETY AT WORK ACT 1974 (HSWA)

The major milestone in the development of legislation in this area was the 1974 Act. All other legislation, both previous and subsequent, is underpinned by HSWA.

The overall aim of the Act is, by taking the right precautions, to prevent people (all workers and members of the public) from being harmed at work.

The specific objectives of the Act are to:

- Secure the health, safety and welfare of all persons at work

- Protect people against the risks arising from workplace activities

- Control the obtaining, keeping and use of explosive or highly flammable substances

- Control emissions into the atmosphere of noxious or offensive substances

49

HEALTH AND SAFETY AT WORK ACT

DUTIES

The Act imposes general duties on all those concerned with health, safety and welfare at work:

- Employers
- Employees
- Manufacturers
- Suppliers
- Designers
- Importers
- Self-employed people
- People in control of premises

We will concentrate on the responsibilities of employers and employees.

HEALTH AND SAFETY

EMPLOYERS' RESPONSIBILITIES

As an **employer** your priorities are to:

1. Make a full assessment of workplace hazards (see later section)
2. Introduce proper controls
3. Monitor their effectiveness

In general terms, your responsibilities are to provide and maintain:

- A safe place of work with safe means of entry and exit
- Safe appliances, equipment and plant for doing the work
- A safe system for doing the work
- Competent and safety-conscious personnel

You are also obliged to provide the information, instruction, training and supervision necessary to ensure the health and safety of your employees (and, in some instances, non-employees).

EMPLOYEES' RESPONSIBILITIES

It is the duty of every **employee** while at work:

- To take reasonable care of their own health and safety as well as that of other persons with whom they may come into contact
- To co-operate as far as is necessary to enable the employer to comply with health and safety duties or requirements

If you are a director, manager, company secretary or other officer of an organisation, you have both general and specific duties under HSWA. Serious breaches of these duties could result in you being prosecuted and even imprisoned.

HEALTH AND SAFETY POLICIES

If you employ at least five members of staff, you need to prepare a written policy statement concerning the arrangements for health and safety at work.

Your health and safety policy should:

- Comply with legislation, eg a smoking ban will apply to workplaces from the end of 2007
- Be tailored to your organisational circumstances
- Contain a general statement of policy concerning health and safety
- Include the arrangements for implementing the policy, including emergencies
- Identify specific hazards and state the rules designed to deal with these
- Clarify how safety rules are communicated to employees and visitors on site

HEALTH AND SAFETY POLICIES

Your policy should also:

- Indicate training and safety provisions for new workers and others
- Register the regular checks and inspections that are needed
- Be periodically reviewed
- Identify the positions of persons for overseeing its implementation

Extract from a policy statement:

HEALTH AND SAFETY POLICY STATEMENT

Maintaining a healthy and safe working environment is an integral part of our business and something we all need to take seriously. The management of health and safety is the responsibility of directors and managers, but it is important that all members of staff, contractors and visitors recognise their responsibility to support and maintain this policy.

We are committed to good levels of safety performance..............

HEALTH AND SAFETY

REPRESENTATIVES AND COMMITTEES

Under HSWA you are obliged to consult on health and safety matters with union-appointed representatives, or, in non-unionised environments, with employee representatives.

The main functions of safety representatives are to:

- Investigate hazards, dangerous occurrences and accidents at the workplace
- Investigate complaints by employees relating to heath, safety and welfare
- Make representations to the employer on the above and on any general issues
- Carry out inspections of the workplace
- Represent employees in consultation with the health and safety authorities
- Attend meetings of safety committees

You must allow the necessary time off work with pay to enable safety representatives to fulfil their duties and to undergo appropriate training. You must also provide appropriate information.

If a request for its establishment is received from at least two safety representatives, you must set up a safety committee within three months. The composition should allow for representation of management and all employees.

HEALTH AND SAFETY REGULATIONS

Over the years regulations have been issued under HSWA covering the specific health and safety requirements on topics such as the ones listed.

You should obtain copies of the appropriate HSE guidance booklets for more information.

- First aid
- Noise at work
- Fire precautions
- Electricity at work
- Control of asbestos at work
- Control of lead at work
- Reporting of injuries, diseases and dangerous occurrences (RIDDOR)
- Control of substances hazardous to health (COSHH)
- Provision and use of work equipment
- Personal protective equipment
- Display screen equipment
- Manual handling

HEALTH AND SAFETY

RISK ASSESSMENT

The Management of Health and Safety at Work Regulations 1992 state that you must:

1. Assess the workplace risks to your employees and others
2. Identify the measures needed to comply with health and safety laws
3. Appoint competent people to help you take the necessary measures

Your risk assessments should be systematic, for example:

Hazard	Risk	Action
Trailing cables	Slips, trips and falls	Use cable tidies

They should cover all the health risks in the workplace, eg:

- Chemical agents
- Other hazardous substances (dust, fumes)
- Noise
- Vibration
- Radiation

- Repetitive movement
- Static/awkward postures
- Infectious diseases
- Manual handling
- Work related stress

Please note that specific provisions and restrictions apply to pregnant and young workers.

EMPLOYMENT PROTECTION

It is the right of safety representatives to be given information and the necessary time off work to fulfil their duties. In addition, you should note that it is automatically unfair to dismiss employees (regardless of the hours of work, length of service or age) for any of the following reasons:

- Taking appropriate steps to protect themselves or others in circumstances of serious or imminent danger
- Performing health and safety responsibilities designated by their employer
- Leaving a dangerous part of the workplace if there is believed to be some serious or imminent danger which could not be averted, or refusing to return while the danger persists
- Bringing a reasonable health and safety concern to their employer's attention in the absence of a representative or relevant committee
- Performing functions as employer-acknowledged safety representatives or as committee members

RELATED EMPLOYMENT POLICIES

Once you have established a good base of effective health and safety policies and practices, you should ensure that there is integration with related employment policies and procedures on areas such as:

Alcohol and drugs
Smoking (see p53)
Stress management
Home working
Health education and promotion
Disciplinary procedures
Ill-health and capability procedures
Grievance procedures
Bullying and harassment
Whistleblowing

If you fail to do this, unforeseen consequences may result. For instance, if you turn a blind eye when it is clear that an employee has a drinking problem then you could be deemed to be in breach of your health and safety duties. Further, ignoring an employee's complaint about the detrimental effect of his/her workload on his/her health could lead to a personal injury claim.

HEALTH AND SAFETY

PENALTIES FOR NON-COMPLIANCE

The three main headings under which you could find yourself subject to legal action are:

1. **A breach of HSWA and associated regulations** – eg failing to carry out a risk assessment under the COSHH regulations could result in the offender (organisation and/or individual) being taken to court and, if found guilty, fined and/or imprisoned.

2. **A breach of common law** – eg if an employee is injured in the workplace as a result of another employee's negligence, the injured party has the right to sue the employer as well as, or instead of, the wrongdoing employee. This is known as vicarious liability. The case will be heard in a civil court and, if successful, damages will be awarded to the injured party.

3. **Unfair dismissal** – claims alleging unfair (including constructive) dismissal and breaches of employment contract terms are heard by employment tribunals. Awards include re-instatement or re-engagement, but compensation is the more likely outcome of a successful claim.

HSE officers also have enforcement powers and if, say, a dangerous occurrence is reported, they can issue improvement notices (detailing the changes required within a timeframe) or prohibition notices (which curtail the activities in question).

WORKING WITH
TRADE UNIONS

TRADE UNIONS AND COLLECTIVE AGREEMENTS

What is a trade union? It is an association of employees, sometimes those who work in a single trade. To be a **trade union** it must be recognised by the Government's Certification Officer as being independent of an employer. It will usually be a member of the TUC.

- You cannot discriminate against employees who join a trade union or engage in their activities – and don't discriminate against non-members, eg by a lower pay rise

- Employers can negotiate their employees' terms and conditions with a trade union. This means they **recognise** the trade union for this purpose (see next page)

- Agreements between employer and trade union are negotiated for a collection of employees – the union members; hence the terms **collective** bargaining and **collective** agreements

- Substantive agreements relate to terms and conditions of employment

- Procedural agreements, unsurprisingly, cover procedures, such as handling redundancies

See the Trade Union and Labour Relations (Consolidation) Act (TULR(C)A) 1992.

TRADE UNION RECOGNITION

Employers of 21 or more people may be obliged to recognise a trade union or, rather than be compelled, they may recognise one voluntarily. Recognition needs to be set out in an agreement. This should cover matters such as:

- How shop stewards are to be elected; they cannot appoint themselves, of course
- How disputes will be resolved
- How negotiations will be conducted
- The union's role in discipline and grievance

It will also determine the **bargaining unit**, that is the group of employees for which the employer recognises the trade union as having negotiating rights. Typically, this may be a single factory or a particular type of employee (eg salaried staff below managerial level).

The agreement's **scope** determines what may be negotiated. For voluntary recognition this may be pay, working hours and holidays only or be extended by agreement to include issues such as overtime pay and arrangements, redundancy selection procedures, etc.

It is unlikely that the average manager will be involved in the negotiation of such an agreement, although it could apply to a small employer of 21 or more people.

WORKING WITH TRADE UNIONS

CONSULTATION RIGHTS

Terms and conditions: Organisations agree to negotiate these, or at least some of these, when they recognise a union.

Training: Union Learning Representatives are entitled to paid time off for their duties. Larger European organisations must consult under European Works Council regulations.

Redundancy: Unions (or, where there is no recognised union, employee representatives) have to be consulted in good time with a view to avoiding or reducing redundancies. See the greater detail in the section on Redundancy.

Transfer of Undertakings Regulations: Organisations must consult trade unions when envisaged that part of an organisation will be transferred under these regulations.

Health and safety: Unions can require organisations to set up safety committees and safety representatives, and to consult with them (see Health and Safety section).

Pensions: Larger employers must consult unions or employee representatives over proposed changes to work-based pensions.

Business's economic situation, employment prospects and related decisions:
Employers of 150 or more people* must consult employee representatives
(*100 or more in 2007, 50 or more in 2008).

OTHER TRADE UNION RIGHTS

Remember that the law gives trade union representatives right to paid time off work for their duties, certain rights to consultation, and some protection from dismissal in the form of enhanced awards if dismissed by reason of their trade union duties.

Trade unions traditionally derived much power from being able to inflict damage on an employer by industrial action, striking for example. Nowadays, trade unions have to be careful before they take industrial action. If they do not meet certain criteria, such as holding ballots first, they can face legal action themselves.

CUSTOM AND PRACTICE

Customs and practices are ways of working that grow up over a period of time. For example, it may become customary for workers to extend a 15-minute tea break to 25 minutes, even though no written 'rule' allows it.

When such practices are allowed without check then, legally, such customs can become an 'implied' term of the contract – **they cannot *then* be unilaterally changed**.

Another category is known as **restrictive practices**, which limit management actions, eg a practice whereby if one person is asked to work overtime then the whole team is entitled to work overtime – 'one in, all in'. These practices, too, can creep in gradually.

The legal status of 'custom and practice' can turn such practices into bargaining chips in negotiations.

CHANGING CUSTOM AND PRACTICE

1. **Mutual agreement** – eg following negotiation, both parties agree to change. You may use a 'buy-out' – typically a one off lump sum payment.

2. **By giving the necessary notice** to end the current contract and by offering a new one.

This second option must be a last resort as:

a) You effectively dismiss the employees

b) You then offer a new contract on terms without the restrictive practices

Employees may claim unfair dismissal, or take the new contract under protest – in 'mitigation of their losses'.

For your defence you must have a sound business reason (determined by case law) for dismissal, consult seriously, and offer a new contract that is reasonable. Persuasion must be attempted; never say: *'Take it or leave it'!*

Giving notice can succeed for an employer but should not be undertaken lightly.

TO CONCLUDE

The law regulates union-management activities by:

● Providing for recognition

● Requiring consultation on a wide range of matters

● Allowing custom and practice to have contractual status

The legislation also requires trade unions themselves to be democratic and to follow specific procedures before taking industrial action.

Although interests of employees and employers will inevitably conflict from time to time, both have a stake in the success of the organisation. It is the reconciling of interests that lies behind working with trade unions. As with most management activities, the law is usually only involved when conflict cannot be resolved between the parties.

WORKPLACE PROBLEMS

INDIVIDUAL CONFLICT SITUATIONS

Here, we explore the legal aspects of different types of conflict affecting individuals in the workplace. Conflict or potential conflict situations which impinge on groups of workers are dealt with in the section on Working with Trade Unions.

This section covers:

- **Discipline** – ie conduct issues and performance issues which are within the employee's control (see p76-77 for more information on this distinction)

- **Grievances** – ie where the employee has a complaint against some aspect of your behaviour as the employer. This may include the behaviour of other employees for whom you are vicariously liable

Poor performance which is outside the employee's control and ill-health issues will be dealt with in the section on Attendance and Performance Problems.

EMPLOYMENT TRIBUNAL CLAIMS

There are three types of employment tribunal claim that could arise from poorly handled discipline cases and grievances:

- **Unfair dismissal** – eg where a former employee alleges that you overreacted to an incident or omitted some steps from your company disciplinary procedure

- **Constructive dismissal** – eg where an employee resigns and claims that you failed to protect him or her from racial harassment at work, or that you forced the resignation in some way

- **Wrongful dismissal** (breach of contract) – eg where you dismissed an employee without following a contractual disciplinary procedure or without proper notice

See the section on Dismissal for more information on the first two categories.

WORKPLACE PROBLEMS

EMPLOYMENT RIGHTS

It is useful to think of three levels of law relating to disciplinary and grievance procedures:

Statutory rights: There is a statutory right for employees to be accompanied to disciplinary and grievance hearings. Further, failure of an employer to comply with new statutory procedures could lead to 'automatically unfair dismissal' and increases to any compensation awarded. These rights will apply to all employees including those with less than 12 months' service. See pages 74, 75 and 85 for more information.

Contractual rights: Many public sector organisations, and some others, put disciplinary and grievance procedures into the employment contract. Failure to follow these contractual procedures could lead to breach of contract and unfair dismissal (including constructive dismissal) claims.

ACAS Code of Practice: The Code recommends that procedures be written and provides guidance on their content and operation. If employers follow the Code of Practice, this can be used as evidence that they 'acted reasonably'.

EMPLOYMENT RIGHTS

When operating disciplinary and grievance procedures you should be careful:

- Not to discriminate on any grounds covered by equal opportunities legislation, eg race, gender or disability

- To take account of the Public Interest Disclosure Act 1998 which provides protection from dismissal or detriment for workers who legitimately raise concerns about certain workplace practices, eg health and safety risks

- To ensure that grievances about serious matters, eg harassment and bullying, are dealt with by senior managers or via a separate procedure

73

THE RIGHT OF ACCOMPANIMENT

The companion may address
the hearing in order to:

- Put the worker's case
- Sum up the worker's case
- Respond on the worker's behalf to
  any view expressed at the hearing

'Workers have a statutory right to be accompanied by a fellow worker or trade union official where they are required or invited by their employer to attend certain disciplinary or grievance hearings and when they make a reasonable request to be so accompanied.' ACAS Code.

Whether in a unionised or non-unionised
environment, you should ask for evidence
that **trade union officials** are certified as
trained for this task.

It is good practice to encourage accompaniment at hearings, as this can help them to
proceed in an orderly manner and you do have to respond (positively) if a worker makes
a **reasonable request**. Your response must include delaying the hearing, if necessary,
to allow accompaniment.

WORKPLACE PROBLEMS

THE RIGHT OF ACCOMPANIMENT

In this context:

- **A disciplinary hearing** is one at which you might contemplate action against an employee. This may include consultation over ill-health absence, for example. An 'investigative hearing' (to establish facts) can take place without accompaniment but has to be adjourned before disciplinary action is contemplated.

- **A grievance hearing** is one where the reason for the grievance *'concerns the performance of a duty by an employer in relation to a worker'*. This means that workers can request accompaniment when the grievance relates to your contractual and statutory commitments, eg an equal pay claim, but not to the pursuit of improvements, eg a request for a pay rise (in the absence of a contractual provision). This distinction can be problematic so, in practice, it is usually best to adopt a flexible approach and allow accompaniment for all formal grievances.

CONDUCT V CAPABILITY

Disciplinary procedures are generally designed to deal with misconduct and may be inappropriate for capability issues. Answer the questions below to understand why.

Is it appropriate for you to discipline:

- A long-serving employee who has been absent for a lengthy period due to a genuine sickness?

- A team member who is not coping with his workload and expanded duties following a recent downsizing exercise?

- A newly-appointed employee who is not meeting her performance targets but who is awaiting skills training?

- A member of staff who is under-performing because of a negative attitude to the work?

The answer is 'no' to the first three questions but is 'yes' to the fourth – see the next page for the reasons.

APPROPRIATENESS OF DISCIPLINARY ACTION

The difference is that, in the fourth example, the shortfall in performance is within the individual's control. Thus, disciplinary procedures can be used where the poor performance is due to negligence, lack of application or attitudinal problems. You need to design a separate capability procedure to deal with the other instances (see the section on Attendance and Performance Problems).

In any event, disciplinary action need not be the only outcome of misconduct. You also need to take account of extenuating circumstances. For example, your investigations into an employee's poor timekeeping may reveal that the 'offender' is a previously satisfactory employee whose problems are connected with short-term domestic circumstances. Therefore, you may decide that disciplinary action is inappropriate and, instead, you may wish to agree a temporary change to working hours, or to offer counselling.

This should not be seen as 'putting off the inevitable', as the outcome is likely to be a much more positive one.

DISCIPLINARY RULES

Disciplinary rules set the standards of behaviour and conduct expected in the workplace. Generally they cover areas such as:

- General conduct, eg adhering to the company's dress code
- Security, eg submitting to a request to search desks and lockers
- Health and safety, eg utilising appropriate safety equipment
- Discrimination, eg making promotion decisions based only on 'the ability to do the job'
- Use of company facilities, eg using company-provided mobile phones for business calls only
- Timekeeping and attendance, eg not tampering with clock cards

WORKPLACE PROBLEMS

GROSS MISCONDUCT

You'll be aware that not all misconduct is of equal severity and lesser penalties, eg oral and written warnings, are reserved for minor breaches. So how will employees know which actions are likely to lead to their dismissal?

It is sensible to provide a non-exhaustive list of those offences that will normally be regarded as examples of gross misconduct, justifying summary dismissal. Summary dismissal is dismissal without notice or pay in lieu of notice, and is only justifiable where the employee's action is felt to be so serious that it goes to the root of the employment relationship.

Common examples of gross misconduct include theft, fraud, serious health and safety infringements, fighting, assault, bullying, harassment, discrimination, serious negligence, disloyalty, insubordination or serious breaches of company policies such as those on internet usage.

DISCIPLINARY PROCEDURES

Disciplinary procedures provide guidelines for adherence to the disciplinary rules and set out the method for dealing with infringements. In summary they should allow for:

- The employee charged with misconduct to be informed in writing, in advance, that a disciplinary hearing is taking place and the nature of the precise allegations

- A full investigation by an unbiased individual to establish the facts of the case

- The employee to be given an opportunity to answer the allegations at a private hearing and to challenge any evidence which will be relied upon in reaching a disciplinary decision

- Those conducting the disciplinary hearing to keep an open mind and not prejudge the case

DISCIPLINARY PROCEDURES

They should also allow for:

- Establishment of any mitigating circumstances

- Detailed notes to be made, at the time, relating to all these matters

- An adjournment to consider the evidence, challenges, explanations and mitigation before arriving at a decision, of which the employee is then advised

- A right of appeal against a disciplinary decision to, ideally, a more senior manager who has not previously been involved in the case

NB: The overall aim of disciplinary procedures is to assist employees in improving their conduct, rather than providing the means for managers to dismiss employees lawfully.

TYPES OF GRIEVANCE

Employees may raise grievances about all manner of topics. Sometimes they do not raise formal grievances but make known their complaints in other ways. Examples of the types of issues are:

- The working environment, eg too hot or cold

- Management style or actions, eg abrasive manner

- Personality clashes or other inter-employee disputes, eg arguments over customer service standards

- Refused requests, eg annual leave

- Perceived inequality of treatment, eg a failed promotion application

- Organisational change, eg new working practices

Fair and effective management of employee concerns can significantly contribute to good employee relations. On the other hand, if you handle complaints badly, increased labour turnover, withdrawal of goodwill and resistance to change, to name but a few, may be the result.

GRIEVANCE PROCEDURES

The purpose of grievance procedures is to provide a framework for dealing promptly and fairly with employee complaints. You should remember that it is a brave employee who does raise a grievance and that really you should thank him or her for bringing the problem to your attention.

You need to ensure that your grievance procedure is:

- Aimed at settling matters as closely as possible to the point of origin

- Rapid in its operation to ensure that all grievances are processed in a timely manner

- Fair and unbiased in the investigatory process and its treatment of the employee concerned

- Clear about how and with whom an issue should be raised (and whom next to apply to if the employee is not satisfied)

STATUTORY PROCEDURES

Statutory Disciplinary and Dismissal Procedures (DDPs) and Grievance Procedures (GPs) apply to all employers. The overall aim is to encourage more employees to use internal dispute resolution machinery, eg grievance procedures and appeals against disciplinary, capability and dismissal decisions, rather than resorting to employment tribunals.

They provide a basic framework for employers dealing with individual conflict situations. If you fail to comply with these minimum statutory procedures then any resultant dismissal will be automatically unfair. However, merely complying with them is not enough to ensure fairness. The well-established rules for determining fairness, eg having a fair reason and acting reasonably, will continue to operate.

Furthermore, a failure on the part of the employee or employer to fully utilise the appropriate procedure may result in successful claims for unfair dismissal, or discrimination, being adjusted upwards or downwards, as appropriate.

STATUTORY PROCEDURES – THREE STAGES

There are three stages that must be followed:

Procedure	Disciplinary	Grievance
Step 1	A written statement of the grounds for disciplinary action and an invitation to a meeting	A written statement of the grievance
Step 2	A meeting between the employer and the employee	
Step 3	An appeal meeting	

NB: Your own company procedures are likely to be more detailed but, if you are designing or revising them, you need to ensure that these minimum requirements are met.

WORKPLACE PROBLEMS

GOOD PRACTICES

You must ensure that your workforce is familiar with the content and operation of your disciplinary and grievance procedures. You can do this by:

- Including the subject in your induction programme for new staff
- Making copies of the procedures readily available to all employees
- Providing training for newly appointed managers and refresher training for existing ones
- Publicising revisions to disciplinary rules, eg updating your dress code or internet usage policy
- Making known the results of successfully resolved grievances, eg a change to overtime allocation arrangements, and even, where appropriate, the outcomes of disciplinary investigations

ATTENDANCE AND PERFORMANCE PROBLEMS

UNAUTHORISED ABSENCE

Unauthorised absence is a disciplinary affair – handle it through the disciplinary procedure.

To avoid being disciplined, employees will often claim 'sickness' as the reason for an absence. You may know they are doing so and find this frustrating. But do not dismiss lightly an employee's claim that they were sick.

You need substantial grounds if you are to treat sickness as not genuine and you should have investigated the circumstances thoroughly before you enter the disciplinary route.

You also need to be consistent. Believing one employee and not another (without substantial grounds) will leave you vulnerable to unfair dismissal claims.

Even if you are suspicious of persistent absence, it may be wiser to treat it as persistent short-term sickness. The outcome will invariably be exactly the same.

ATTENDANCE AND PERFORMANCE PROBLEMS

LEGAL ENTITLEMENTS TO TIME OFF

Of course, employees have some legal rights to time off work; here are most of them:

Right	Outline of right, as in 2006
Annual leave	A minimum of 20 days paid leave
Maternity leave (service requirements qualify for additional leave)	Six weeks at 90% of earnings 20 weeks at a statutory rate (SMP) 26 weeks additional – need not be paid
Paternity leave	One week or two consecutive weeks – paid at SMP
Adoption leave	Limited pay
Parental and parental adoption leave	13 weeks per qualifying child – unpaid Rules apply about how you need to allow it
Antenatal care	Reasonable time – paid
Family emergencies	Reasonable time for necessary action – unpaid
Public duties	Reasonable time – need to pay not specified
Union, safety and learning representative duties	Reasonable time for certain duties – paid Union members allowed time for 'activities' – unpaid
Under notice of redundancy	Reasonable time during notice period to job-seek – paid

ATTENDANCE AND PERFORMANCE PROBLEMS

CAPABILITY

- An employee who is genuinely not capable of the required performance should be treated as a capability case rather than be disciplined. Poor performance may be due to a lack of skills, qualifications, training or adequate supervision
- An employee who is genuinely ill should also be managed through a capability procedure
- As suggested earlier, it is usually best to treat illness as genuine unless you have indisputable evidence to the contrary. You can still put pressure on the non-genuine and even dismiss
- You also need to consider people with disabilities who must not be treated unfavourably

Capability issues may arise from an employee's performance, from their attendance or even both. The procedure will be slightly different in each case.

If, in a capability meeting, you anticipate that you might caution an employee that formal action could be taken, you must allow the employee to be accompanied if they request it.

Remember to monitor attendance and performance, and to keep full records, including notes of meetings and return to work interviews. **Your** health may depend on it!

ATTENDANCE AND PERFORMANCE PROBLEMS

DISABILITY DISCRIMINATION ACT 1995

'Workers' including employees, as described in the section Contracts of Employment, are protected from discrimination if they meet this definition:

A person must have, or have had, *'a physical or mental impairment that causes (or caused) a substantial and long-term adverse effect on his or her ability to carry out normal day-to-day activities'*.

More explanation is found in the very readable Code of Practice.

You must not treat such a person less favourably, for a reason related to the disability, than you would treat someone else.

You are under a legal obligation to make reasonable adjustments to ensure that disabled people are not put at any substantial disadvantage. Incidentally, this Act covers all aspects of employment from recruitment to termination and, in some cases, even beyond. See the section on Avoiding Discrimination.

ATTENDANCE AND PERFORMANCE PROBLEMS

CAPABILITY PROCEDURE

POOR PERFORMANCE

Before you consider dismissing by reason of performance, check that you have:

- Asked your employee for an explanation, and checked it as appropriate
- Provided suitable training and given reasonable time to reach the required standard of performance
- Considered suitable alternative work
- Explained the position to the employee, and consulted them for their ideas
- Made sure that a fair and genuine chance to improve has been given
- Provided all 'reasonable adjustments' if the employee has a disability
- Warned the employee that dismissal could result from a failure to improve

If the main cause of poor performance is the changing nature of the job, you might consider whether the situation might properly be treated as a redundancy matter rather than a capability issue.

CAPABILITY PROCEDURE
PERSISTENT SHORT-TERM ABSENCE

You need to act fairly, with an emphasis on consultation.

- Confront the employee with their attendance record to establish the facts behind the absences

- Establish first whether there could be a single underlying cause behind the absences

- If in any doubt, seek permission for a medical report (see page 96)

- If there is a single underlying cause you need to act within the Disability Discrimination Act and use the capability procedure (see next page)

- If the disruption to your business is significant then caution the employee that you cannot continue to tolerate it. Set a time for review; three or six months may be suitable

There should be a rising level of concern shown before you reach the point of dismissal. (This outcome is frequently never reached, because employees often improve their attendance if they can.) There is no reliable guidance as to what level of absence will lead to a fair dismissal.

ATTENDANCE AND PERFORMANCE PROBLEMS

CAPABILITY PROCEDURE
LONGER-TERM ILL-HEALTH OR UNDERLYING CAUSE

If you consider dismissing by reason of ill-health capability, make sure you have first:

- Investigated the facts thoroughly
- Sought medical advice (also critical for short-term absence, if an underlying cause)
- Checked whether the employee has a disability
- Discovered whether a return is possible now
- Assessed if a return is likely in the future, and if so the likely date
- Consulted the employee, outlined your position, listened to and assessed what they want
- Considered all possible alternatives, different hours or work, or reasonable adjustments
- Cautioned dismissal may result if changes cannot be agreed or improvement achieved
- Allowed time for both parties to consider the situation and reviewed it subsequently
- Assessed whether you could keep the job open and if so, for how long. Tribunals may be more understanding if it is crucial that you replace an employee quickly
- Checked you are not breaching the contract or compromising permanent health insurance

The responsibility for keeping in touch with, and consulting, the employee rests with you!

ATTENDANCE AND PERFORMANCE PROBLEMS

MEDICAL REPORTS

Consider whom you will ask for a medical report. A consultant may carry more weight than a general practitioner. A company doctor may have more knowledge of the work involved.

You need an employee's consent before you seek a medical report and you must tell your employee of their rights (in writing, of course):

● To withhold consent to applying for a report in the first place
● To have access to any information before it is sent to you and, in this case:
  - to withhold consent to the report being supplied to you
  - to request changes
  - to have objections (to any changes not made) attached to the report

These rights can affect the time it takes for you to receive the report. The employee can take up to 21 days to view the report and may then request changes. A good case for getting the employee's consent early in the absence!

REQUESTING A MEDICAL REPORT

Your request needs to relate to your employee's health in relation to the job. Unless the report is from a company doctor, you need to tell the doctor about the employee's normal duties and indicate in practical detail the physical and mental demands.

You might ask for professional opinions on:

● The likelihood of a return to work

● When such a return to work might be

● The employee's health in relation to their current duties

● Whether a reduction in the demands of the job would aid a return to work

● Whether that reduction would need to be temporary or permanent

● Information that might be taken into account in considering continued employment

It is a good idea to ask the doctor to examine your employee rather than to compile the report from records.

ATTENDANCE AND PERFORMANCE PROBLEMS

FRUSTRATION!

It is not surprising that managers feel frustrated with absence issues! The issues do require careful management. But there is a different form of frustration.

Some employers like to treat absence, such as an ongoing failure to come to work, as if the contract has been *frustrated*. Beware! Tribunals are reluctant to accept frustration, perhaps because it excludes the employment protection rights associated with dismissal.

It is much wiser to investigate the circumstances fully. If you are precipitate you could later discover that the employee was in hospital – how would that look?

It is also often unwise to treat imprisonment as *frustration of contract*. Choose a fair reason to dismiss instead. It may be appropriate to rely on 'some other substantial reason'. This could be valid if your organisation's business is to install security devices and the employee has been imprisoned for burglary. Take every reasonable step to obtain all the relevant facts, the nature of the offence and the likely period of detention before making a decision.

Sadly, very long prison sentences, and death, are the safest examples of frustrated contracts.

ATTENDANCE AND PERFORMANCE PROBLEMS

YOUR RESPONSIBILITIES

Finally, not all absence or poor performance is the direct responsibility of the employee! You have a responsibility also.

The factors below contribute to absence. Some of them may also make a dismissal unfair if cited in an employment tribunal claim.

- Harassment or bullying and the stress caused by it
- Stress caused by role ambiguity
- Unrewarding work
- Discriminatory practices
- Lack of supervisory training
- An employee's lack of training for his/her responsibilities
- Work overload
- Unhealthy environments
- A failure to provide flexible working arrangements

None of these charges would apply to you, would they?

REDUNDANCY

WHAT IS REDUNDANCY?

Redundancy is one of six potentially fair reasons for dismissal (see p114).

Redundancies occur when an organisation has more employees than it needs to carry out its activities. The Employment Rights Act 1996 refers to:

- A reduction or cessation of work of a particular kind, or
- A reduction or cessation of work of a particular kind at the place where the employee is employed

REDUNDANCY

EMPLOYMENT RIGHTS

Employees have, subject to service eligibility, various rights in connection with redundancy situations, including:

1. The right to statutory redundancy pay.

2. The right not to be unfairly dismissed. For instance, you should not use redundancy as an excuse for sacking poor performers when the real reason for dismissal is capability. You must also follow a fair procedure (see later in this section) in handling redundancy situations.

3. The right not to be unfairly selected for redundancy, eg on the grounds of race, sex, pregnancy or disability.

4. The right to be consulted prior to a redundancy occurring (see over).

5. The right to a trial period of four weeks if offered suitable alternative employment.

6. The right, during notice of redundancy, to take a reasonable amount of paid time off during working hours to look for new employment or to arrange employment-related training.

CONSULTATION

There is a legal obligation for you, as an employer, to consult with trade union or employee representatives in redundancy situations.

This process should begin at least 90 days or 30 days (depending on the numbers involved) before the first dismissal takes effect. (These timings tie in with the legal requirements for employers to notify the Secretary of State for Trade and Industry of large-scale redundancies – see the Dti guide on redundancy consultation and notification listed in the Further Reading section for more details.)

Case law dictates that you should also consult with all the individuals likely to be affected by proposed redundancies. Otherwise any resultant dismissals could be deemed to be unfair. (See later in this section for tips on 'breaking the bad news'.)

REDUNDANCY

CONTENT AND PURPOSE OF CONSULTATION

The content of collective consultations should centre on discussions about:

- The reasons for proposed redundancies
- The numbers and categories of employees likely to be involved
- The proposed method of selection for redundancy (see page 106)
- The proposed method and timing of dismissals
- The method of calculating redundancy payments
  (over and above statutory entitlements)

But more importantly, the purpose of all
consultations (collective and individual)
is to consider:

- Ways to avoid the dismissals
  and reduce the number of
  employees to be made
  redundant (see next section)

THE AIM IS TO REDUCE THE IMPACT OF REDUNDANCY

OR AVOID IT ALTOGETHER

AVOIDING REDUNDANCY

As well as looking at other cost-cutting initiatives, the measures you should consider for minimising or avoiding compulsory redundancies include:

- Natural wastage
- A recruitment freeze
- Retraining or redeployment to other parts of the business or an associated business (see next section)
- Reduction or elimination of overtime working
- Introduction of short-time working or temporary lay-off (if provided for in the contract of employment)
- Retirement of those already at or beyond the default retirement age of 65
- Seeking applications for early retirement or voluntary redundancy
- Termination of the employment of contract staff

SUITABLE ALTERNATIVE EMPLOYMENT

If you make an offer of suitable alternative employment to a redundant employee before the end of the contract, you can avoid making a redundancy payment. The offer may involve a different type of work or different terms of employment, eg hours of work, pay, status, location. Obviously opinions may vary on the suitability of the employment offered, but open and honest consultations should help you to reach a shared understanding.

If an employee refuses such an offer or resigns during the trial period, you could refuse to make a redundancy payment. If an employment tribunal claim was subsequently received, you would need to show that the alternative work was suitable and the employee's rejection of it was unreasonable.

REDUNDANCY SELECTION CRITERIA

If compulsory redundancies cannot be avoided then you will need to agree a fair and objective method for selecting the employees who will be made redundant. You may wish to consider choosing an appropriate combination of criteria from the following list, as relying too heavily on one or two could lead to discrimination claims. This list contains examples only and is not intended to be definitive:

- LIFO – last in, first out (be aware of the age discrimination implications of this choice)
- Attendance/absence records (care is needed to avoid disability and pregnancy-related discrimination)
- Performance on measurable and objective criteria
- Disciplinary records
- Qualifications relevant to the work
- Identifiable skills or knowledge needed in the business

You will then need to decide on a systematic method of rating employees against the criteria. Also, will some of the criteria be more heavily weighted than others to reflect their varying importance to the future needs of the business?

REDUNDANCY

FOLLOWING A FAIR PROCEDURE

It is a good idea to draw up a redundancy policy and procedure (and agree it with the trade union, where appropriate) well in advance of a potential redundancy situation. The following checklist shows the good practice steps you should employ:

- Comply with all your legal obligations
- Begin consultations as early as possible with representatives, where applicable, and with individual employees
- Ensure that consultations are entered into in good faith with a view to reaching agreement
- Give serious consideration and respond to the views of representatives and/or employees, particularly where their suggestions could avoid or minimise redundancies
- Agree non-discriminatory and workable redundancy selection criteria
- Be objective, fair and consistent in applying the criteria and in hearing appeals against selection
- Actively explore opportunities for suitable alternative work during the notice period
- Consider other ways of helping redundant employees by, say, offering enhanced redundancy payments and/or providing access to financial advice, help with job hunting and counselling services

REDUNDANCY

BREAKING THE BAD NEWS

Consulting with those likely to be affected by redundancy plans is accepted good practice. The way in which you break the bad news is very important. As well as complying with the legal requirements you need to ensure a sensitive and humane approach.

Following the tips below should help:

- Prepare not only what you are going to say but also for any questions the employee may have, eg notice, payment and other legal entitlements, the implications regarding other company benefits

- Choose a suitable venue for the meeting and think through the timing and logistics. For instance, if the employee is upset, will s/he be expected to go straight back to the office?

- Notify the employee of the right of accompaniment/representation

- Get to the point and warn the employee that his or her job is at risk and explain the reason for the redundancy situation and why he or she has potentially been selected

BREAKING THE BAD NEWS

- Engage in genuine consultation, ie be open-minded about alternatives to redundancy and redeployment opportunities
- Empathise but ensure that your message is understood
- Be prepared to adjourn if necessary, eg to allow for thinking time or because emotions are running high
- Have a second management representative in attendance at each meeting, wherever possible, to act as a witness and note-taker
- Set a review date for future meetings and confirm the results of each meeting in writing
- Should dismissal be the ultimate outcome, notify the employee of the mechanism for appeal – see also the section on Dismissing Employees

NOTES

DISMISSING EMPLOYEES

WHAT IS A DISMISSAL?

1. You, the employer, terminate the contract of employment.
2. A fixed term contract expires and you decide not to renew it. This is still a dismissal and you may have to show it to be fair, as with other dismissals.
3. An employee terminates his/her own contract of employment because you have acted so as to breach the contract (constructive dismissal), eg you assault an employee.

In these cases you must ask yourself:

- Do I have a fair reason and am I acting fairly in reaching a decision to dismiss?
- Does the employee have unfair dismissal rights (see below)?

Other points:
Frustration of contract is not a dismissal nor is termination by mutual agreement. However, it would be wise to take further advice before you assume either of these apply.

True resignation is not a dismissal but, if you can, check that it is not a constructive dismissal before accepting it. In the latter case, you might take remedial action, if it is not too late.

UNFAIR DISMISSAL RIGHTS

Employees with 12 months' service have the right 'to not be dismissed unfairly'. Irrespective of service, the following are examples of reasons for dismissal that could also give rise to claims:

- Pregnancy
- Trade union membership (or non-membership)
- Activities or duties as a statutory employee representative
- Failure to follow an instruction to carry out an unsafe practice
- Refusal to work on a Sunday by a shop worker
- Asserting a statutory right, see the section on Avoiding Discrimination for examples
- Exercise of a number of rights, eg national minimum wage and working time

Additionally, anti-discrimination legislation protects employees and job applicants on specified grounds, eg sex, race. An employee who thinks that they have been treated unfairly may make a claim to an employment tribunal for compensation.

As you can see, legislation protects many employees against unfair dismissal. So before you consider dismissing an employee make sure, first, that you have a fair reason.

DISMISSING EMPLOYEES

FAIR REASON

You can only dismiss someone fairly for one of the following reasons:

Conduct – failure to meet reasonable expectations. See also Workplace problems.

Capability – inability to perform the type of work for which the employee was employed. See also Attendance and Capability.

Redundancy – the work for which the employee was employed has ceased or diminished. See also Redundancy.

Legal restrictions – that make it unlawful for the employee to continue to work in the position, eg where a work permit expires or a driving licence is lost.

'Some other substantial reason' – reasons established by precedents in case law, eg a serious and relevant breakdown in trust due to the employee's conduct outside work, or where there are sound business reasons, eg a reorganisation.

Retirement – (from October 2006) of a worker because he or she has reached age 65 (or is over the age of 65). The dismissal must be genuinely due to retirement.

DISMISSAL BY REASON OF CONDUCT

Conduct

This can relate to the employee's behaviour or performance. However, it should refer only to behaviour or performance that is within your employee's capability, ie low performance or unsuitable behaviour because the employee is just not trying, rather than is not capable.

Dismissals for conduct must never be for the first offence (unless the offence is gross misconduct). That means following the stages in your disciplinary procedure.

Gross misconduct

See the section on Workplace Problems for examples of gross misconduct offences. In such instances you should dismiss without any notice pay, because the employee has broken the contract (and you need no longer be bound by it).

Like all conduct cases, you need to carry out a full investigation and conduct a fair hearing before you take the decision. You should consider suspending your employee on full pay while these activities take place.

The section on Workplace Problems has details of fair procedures for discipline and dismissal.

CONSTRUCTIVE DISMISSAL

This is like the opposite side of the coin to gross misconduct, only here it is you, the employer, who has broken the contract.

For instance, if you humiliate an employee in front of his or her direct reports you may make it impossible for that person to continue working for you. You break the contract (because employer and employee need to agree to co-operate with each other) and the employee considers himself/herself dismissed.

Constructive dismissals are a headache. If dismissal is established, how do you show that you acted fairly when it was your inappropriate action that caused the dismissal?

On the other hand such dismissals can be hard to establish in a tribunal. The employee has to show that your behaviour was not just inappropriate, or made without agreement, but that it went to the 'root of the contract'.

This means that, in practice, you may be able to change some minor aspects of the contract, provided the variation is reasonable, eg a small change in the exact place of work.

DISMISSING EMPLOYEES

DISMISSAL FOR CAPABILITY

Remember, if a dismissal has to take place, that it is not the employee's 'fault' that they are not capable. Always providing that you have taken reasonable steps, offering training or adjustments in appropriate cases, it is not your 'fault' either.

Dismissal should be with the appropriate notice and it is important to note that this applies even if the employee is off on long-term sickness and no longer in receipt of sickness payments.

We covered the procedure which you should follow in the section on Attendance and Performance Problems.

DISMISSING EMPLOYEES

DISMISSAL BY REASON OF REDUNDANCY

Employees with two or more years' service are entitled to a statutory redundancy payment (subject to an upper limit). Details can be found in various publications listed in the Further Reading section.

Unless you intend that the employees will work out their notice (unusual since their work is diminished and their motivation will be minimal) you need to make payments in lieu of notice. Such payments probably need tax to be deducted but this is a matter of detailed Inland Revenue rules. You should check with the IR enquiry line before paying out in lieu of notice.

If your organisation pays out enhanced redundancy payments (ie above the statutory minimum) there may well be tax implications and again you need to make checks before making payments.

The procedures to be followed and the question of breaking the news are covered in the section on Redundancy.

DISMISSAL BECAUSE OF LEGAL RESTRICTIONS

If an employee of yours needs a legal qualification (eg a driving licence) to carry out his or her job and loses that qualification, it may be possible to dismiss him or her fairly.

However, you will still need to show that you have acted fairly, in all the circumstances, in treating this as a sufficient reason for dismissal. The same general principles of obtaining the facts, considering alternatives and consulting the employee (accompanied if a request is made) apply here as they do in other hearings.

Fairness is likely to rest heavily on the circumstances, eg:

- As the director of a small collection and delivery company you may be able to justify dismissing an employee who is disqualified from driving
- As the manager of a large distribution warehouse you could be expected to offer a disqualified driver a warehouse position during any driving ban

DISMISSAL FOR SOME OTHER SUBSTANTIAL REASON

These reasons usually relate to conduct outside work and sometimes to matters outside the individual's direct control.

Example 1

An employee in a position of high trust who then proves to be a thief in some outside situation might be dismissed. It would be a substantial reason if your organisation has no positions available for someone of such a dishonest disposition. However, if you did have such positions available you might not be able to defend the dismissal.

Example 2

An employee's wife goes to work for your main competitor. In some circumstances you may be able to dismiss the employee for the substantial reason of protecting your business.

In these cases it does not necessarily follow that your employee has broken their contract. Therefore it would be appropriate to pay the employee notice.

Fairness can be difficult to show because disciplinary procedures are not appropriate. Nonetheless you need to hear the employee's side of the story, allowing accompaniment, before you reach a decision.

DISMISSAL FOR SOME OTHER SUBSTANTIAL REASON

Example 3

A team of fire-extinguisher maintenance engineers is re-organised and given a new task. Engineers now have to sell extinguishers as well as service them. Usually they would be persuaded to accept the new task and thereby agree a change in their contract terms. But what if they object? It is a basic principle of a contract that one party (eg the employer) cannot change it without the agreement of the other party (the employee). Fundamental changes, if imposed, may amount to constructive dismissal.

One option for the employer is to dismiss all the engineers and offer them new contracts as 'Sales Engineers'. The intention would be, of course, that the engineers would accept the new contracts. But if they do not and if the employer has **a sound business reason** for doing this, the dismissals may be found to be fair. The basis would be 'some other substantial reason'.

However, this is a complex area and fraught with potential difficulties. You will need advice or substantial further reading before choosing this option.

DISMISSAL – WHAT YOU MIGHT SAY

If, after following a full procedure, dismissal is decided on, you need to tell your employee. Prepare, in advance, what you will say; draft out the key points. It is important to own your decision, so in the meeting do not then read out what you have written. Explain your position, following the general line of your preparation and taking care to cover each point. Note any changes afterwards and keep your annotated notes as a record of what was said.

The main points you are likely to want to cover are:

- The substance of any explanations offered by your employee
- That despite these explanations and any mitigating circumstances (mention any that you have taken into account), you have reached the decision to dismiss
- If appropriate (eg in disability cases), alternatives that you have considered
- In redundancy, you might outline the process that has brought you to this position
- The reason that you have arrived at your decision
- Arrangements for notice or pay in lieu of notice, *if appropriate*
- Arrangements for leaving the premises, *as appropriate*
- Any right to appeal and what s/he should do if they want to exercise it
- The fact that they are dismissed – do not allow for doubt

DISMISSING EMPLOYEES

APPEALS

- Ask the grounds for the appeal – eg have new facts appeared or is the penalty felt to be too harsh?

- Appeals should be heard after time for reflection (a few days), but reasonably promptly

- If possible, a more senior manager should hear any appeal. If you are the boss of a small firm, allow time and then 'look at it again'. You need to be as impartial as possible

- The employee has the right of accompaniment at an appeal hearing

- Structure the appeal around the stated grounds for the appeal, eg if it is only the severity of the penalty that is questioned, focus on that aspect

- If you uphold the appeal explain the reasons to the managers involved, as appropriate. They may need support or training

- If you dismiss the appeal, you need to make it clear that the decision is final or, if not, the means for pursuing it further

FURTHER READING

Contracts of Employment
Drawing up Employment Contracts, Olga Aikin, CIPD

Avoiding Discrimination
Code of Practice: Equal opportunities policies, procedures and practices in employment, TSO
Code of Practice: For the elimination of discrimination in the field of employment against disabled persons or persons who have had a disability, TSO
Code of Practice on Equal Pay
Code of Practice: For the elimination of racial discrimination and the promotion of equality of opportunity in employment
Age Diversity In Employment: A Code of Practice
Fair Employment (Northern Ireland) Code of Practice

Control and Administration
A Guide to the Working Time Regulations, Department of Trade and Industry
A Detailed Guide to the National Minimum Wage, Department of Trade and Industry
The Employment Practices Data Protection Code

FURTHER READING

Working with Trade Unions
Employees' information and consultation rights on collective redundancies and transfers of undertakings: A short guide to the new requirements, Department of Trade and Industry
Trade Union & Labour Relations (Consolidation) Act (TULR(C)A) 1992, HMSO

Health and Safety
An Introduction to Health and Safety (INDG 259), HSE Books
Health & Employment: Advisory Booklet, ACAS

Workplace Problems
Bullying and Harassment at Work - guide for managers and employers, advice leaflet
Drugs and Alcohol Policies, Tricia Jackson, CIPD
Smoking Policies, Tricia Jackson, CIPD
Discipline and Grievances at Work: Advisory Handbook, ACAS
Handling Discipline, Tricia Jackson, CIPD
Handling Grievances, Tricia Jackson, CIPD
Bullying and Sexual Harassment, Tina Stephens, CIPD
The Discipline Pocketbook, Stuart Emmett, Management Pocketbooks

FURTHER READING

Attendance Problems

Positive Attendance Management, Bill McCulloch, PPP Healthcare
From Absence to Attendance (Developing Practice), Alastair Evans, Mike Walters, CIPD
The Controlling Absenteeism Pocketbook, Max A. Eggert, Management Pocketbooks

Redundancy

Managing Redundancy, Alan Fowler, (CIPD)
Redundancy Consultation & Notification, PL833, Department of Trade and Industry
Redundancy Handling: Advisory Booklet, ACAS

Websites

Most of the above publications can be downloaded or ordered from these sites:

Arbitration, Conciliation and Advisory Service (ACAS)	www.acas.org.uk
Chartered Institute of Personnel and Development (CIPD)	www.cipd.co.uk
Department of Trade and Industry (DTI)	www.dti.gov.uk/er/index.htm
Health and Safety Executive (HSE)	www.hsebooks.co.uk
Her Majesty's Stationery Office (HMSO)	www.hmso.gov.uk
Information Commissioner (Data Protection)	www.informationcommissioner.gov.uk
Management Pocketbooks	www.pocketbook.co.uk
The Stationery Office (TSO)	www.tso-online.co.uk

About the Authors

Malcolm Martin BSc MCMI Chartered FCIPD is Managing Director of Employer Solutions Ltd. His experience is in a range of sectors from care, education and manufacturing, to polymers, chemicals and steel. Early in his career he spent time on the shop floor and subsequently trained supervisors, line and HR managers, and shop stewards in industrial relations. Prior to starting in business he held middle management positions in industrial relations, project management and human resources. He has been successfully examined, and holds a University Certificate, in Employment Law.

Employer Solutions Limited prepares employee handbooks for small and medium sized organisations and delivers training and consultancy services in employment practices, providing rich experience for this book.

Contact: malcolm@employersolutions.co.uk

Tricia Jackson, BA MSc Chartered FCIPD MInstAM Diploma in Employment Law (distinction), is a freelance consultant and tutor in personnel and development as well as an enthusiastic writer. She provides tailor-made training solutions and HR consultancy services to a wide range of employing organisations.

Tricia has represented clients successfully at employment tribunals. She is heavily involved in educating and encouraging managers to improve their knowledge and understanding of legislative provisions and to adopt good practices (thereby minimising the likelihood of tribunal claims). She is also a qualified mediator.

Tricia co-authored, with Malcolm, the best-selling book Personnel Practice, published by the CIPD. She has also written five books in the CIPD Good Practice series including Handling Grievances and Handling Discipline.

Contact: triciajack@aol.com

ORDER FORM

Your details

Name _____

Position _____

Company _____

Address _____

_____

Telephone _____

Fax _____

E-mail _____

VAT No. (EC companies) _____

Your Order Ref _____

Please send me:

		No. copies
The Employment Law	Pocketbook	
The _____	Pocketbook	
The _____	Pocketbook	
The _____	Pocketbook	
The _____	Pocketbook	

Order by Post
MANAGEMENT POCKETBOOKS LTD
LAUREL HOUSE, STATION APPROACH,
ALRESFORD, HAMPSHIRE SO24 9JH UK

Order by Phone, Fax or Internet
Telephone: +44 (0)1962 735573
Facsimile: +44 (0)1962 733637
E-mail: sales@pocketbook.co.uk
Web: www.pocketbook.co.uk

MANAGEMENT POCKETBOOKS